WENDIGO WOODS

ANTLERS IN THE MIST

A recount by
Jessica Young
and
Tom Lyons

WENDIGO WOODS: ANTLERS IN THE MIST

Copyright © 2020 Jessica Young and Tom Lyons

All rights reserved. No part of this may be reproduced without the consent of the authors, except brief quotes used in reviews.

All information and opinions expressed in *Wendigo Woods: Antlers in the Mist* are entirely the author's and are based upon Jessica's perspective and experiences. She does not purport the information presented in this book is based on any accurate, current, or valid scientific knowledge.

Acknowledgments

It's certainly not an easy task for someone to discuss their terrifying encounters with cryptids. Thank you to those who found the courage to tell their experiences.

To respect those who were involved, all of the following names have been altered to protect their privacy. Also, things like restaurants and street names were changed.

Contents

Introduction 5
Chapter 1...10
Chapter 2...24
Chapter 3...34
Chapter 4...41
Chapter 5...49
Chapter 6...54
Chapter 7...66
Chapter 8...79
Chapter 9...87
Conclusion 97
Another Popular Series 99
Author's Note 101
Mailing List Sign Up Form 103
Social Media 105
About the Author 107

A Word from Tom

My intuition tells me that, before anything else, I should warn you that you're about to begin what I found to be an extraordinarily unsettling story. If you've read any or all of my previous work, you probably know not to take that statement lightly; those words should find a way to resonate. Nevertheless, the following report instantly grabbed my attention. If you're aware of the basic details of my experience with the sasquatch species, you'd be right to suspect that I need some thrilling material to motivate me to write an entire series. It was as soon as Jessica reached out to me that I knew she had provided me with another gem.

What I especially like about this tale is how it involves an entity that is so overwhelmingly mysterious, that I'm surprised it's not a more popular topic for conversation. But, then again, how is it that the sasquatch species, something that is so blatantly real, has only recently started gaining momentum as socially acceptable subject matter? I think those notions alone are sufficient in emphasizing just how strange this existence is. I mean, consider the spectrum of topics that we face daily. Is it not at all unsettling to you how so much of our society cares more about Kim Kardashian's latest outfit rather than the most recent UFO reports, a few of which have been mentioned by the United States government? I do prefer to be a sympathetic individual, but I admit I find it challenging not to laugh at the stupidity of that sad reality. There's no question that forces are striving to preserve the ignorance of humanity. But we can't blame them entirely; at the end of the day, I believe it's our responsibility to decide when enough is enough. It's up to us to reject the seemingly never-ending abyss of nonsense that is spewed upon us every day. That's why I believe it's so important to regularly immerse yourself in nature in order to obtain mental clarity. When you acquire some of that clarity, you open your senses to the realm of possibility. In other words, you disregard so many of the silly claims by pop culture, and you see that this existence is so much more complicated than many of us have been led to believe.

I sure do appreciate every occasion where an individual like Jessica reaches out to me about their mysterious experience with the unknown. Each time that happens, my sense of community grows, and it's a reminder that my own experience isn't as unusual as I had once thought. Happy reading, everyone.

-Tom

Introduction

I was delighted. That's the perfect word to express how I felt when my husband, Anthony, and I, decided to move to Cape Elizabeth, Maine, back in 2012. We had been living in Nashville, Tennessee, for just under a decade, and the thought of moving to the coast was entirely attractive. My name is Jessica. To give you a better idea of what I look like, I'm 5'8" tall, weigh about 120 lbs, and have brown eyes and dark brown shoulder-length hair. My husband is about 5'11" tall. He has a slim build, dark blonde hair, and blue eyes. I spent the majority of my childhood in Charleston, South Carolina, and there was something very appealing about the idea of our two children, Madeline and Kellen, experiencing life near the sea. Madeline was nine years old and has always been passionate about reading and writing. She has always shown intelligence beyond her years, but she could also be somewhat stubborn and argumentative. Although we loved her so very much, her sometimes snide attitude would lead to tension between her father and I. We would often get in arguments when he'd try to comfort her after I'd scold her for talking back. But I'd have to remind myself that Anthony's demanding workload disallowed him from spending as much time with his kids as he would've liked. That was never anything I held against him; after all, it was his career as a top financial advisor that provided us with a life of luxury. And it was always transparent that he genuinely wanted to be more involved in the lives of his children, so I never felt the right to accuse him of anything otherwise.

Kellen had just turned six. Compared to most children, he was easy to please. All we'd have to do was hand him a *Star Wars* picture book or toy, and he'd sit down to quietly entertain himself for hours at a time. Fortunately, Madeline seemed to understand her role as the caring older sister; she was protective of her little brother from the second he was born. I sure did appreciate that about my daughter.

Both of our children seemed content with the move. Part of the reason for that was that they were too young and weren't given enough time to develop a lasting attachment to the city of Nashville. Plus, I think Anthony and I did a stellar job at talking up Cape Elizabeth. We probably made it sound like a land out of a fairytale. When considering the future events, that notion wasn't very far off; although, it ended up being much more of a nightmarish fairytale than a happy one.

I sincerely appreciate you taking the time to read about my family's experience with the paranormal. Some of my actions throughout the story will likely make you feel embarrassed or uncomfortable; therefore, I ask that you grant me the benefit of the doubt and save any harsh judgments until after you've completed the series.

    -Jessica

Chapter 1

The search had begun to feel stale; we must've strolled through nearly twenty different homes, and not a single one seemed to speak to either one of us. Things felt even more challenging because our discussions were constantly interrupted by phone calls from Anthony's clients. My husband loved his work, and he was very skilled at it, but it was one of those careers that nearly required 24-hour attention. When thinking about it, it's a bit ironic how many of our conversations regarding how to invest our own money were cut off by people who want to talk about that very same thing. Additionally, I was stricken by the laziness of each of the local realtors that we had worked with. By that point, I believe we had gone through about four of them, all of which were very nice but always very late. I couldn't make any sense of it; surely, it was just a spree of bad luck.

The kids had been staying with Anthony's parents just outside of Nashville. Our kids loved their grandparents, Grace and Mitchell, dearly, and they loved them back, but I felt like the constant babysitting had begun to exhaust them. My husband's parents were as pleasant and generous as they come, but the majority of their daily living was spent reading novels in their den. They had grown accustomed to a tranquil life that most young children, even the well-behaved ones, don't mesh very well with. That was another source of motivation to finish the house hunt. It had gotten to the point where we probably would've called the move off, or at least postponed it if it hadn't been for the fact that we were so passionate about the idea.

I remember it was on a Sunday afternoon that we were about to quit the search for the day when we drove past an open house sign on the way back to our rental house.

"Pinewood Lane," I read aloud as we slowed down to check out the sign. "Has a nice ring to it, don't you think?"

Our expectations were by no means high, given the fact that the listing hadn't been suggested to us, but we figured we had nothing to lose. Strangely enough, it was as we turned onto the property's street that I was seduced by charm. The reason I say that is because there was nothing yet visible other than rows of the same kinds of trees we had been observing for hours. It was an invisible charm that made me feel a sense of belonging. After we drove what was probably a quarter of a mile up the street, I was awestruck by a view of the sea through the trees. We switched off the air conditioning and rolled down the windows, only to be further entranced by the echoes of crashing waves.

"I think we already know that this is going to be way out of our price range," Anthony chuckled, "that's why there was no mention of the place." Although, I couldn't help but agree with his logic, that strange feeling that insisted this could be our new home persisted.

After we continued the slow drive toward the ocean, it wasn't much longer before we saw the entrance to the driveway that was accompanied by two stone pillars and bright green shrubbery. As far as we could see, there wasn't a sign that stated this was the property up for sale; nevertheless, we decided to take our chances and pull in. It truly felt as though gravity had pulled me toward the place. And bear in mind that I wasn't even the one driving.

To say the house looked magnificent wouldn't do it justice. Sure, it needed some work, but it was the exact type of place that I could envision our kids safely running around for years to come. Lush grass surrounded the blacktop driveway that looped around an old stone water fountain that was shaped like a little boy and his dog standing beside one another. The closer we got to the house, the more apparent it became that there was a separate guest house positioned to the left of what had to be a very spacious backyard. The guest house, alone, would've been perceived as excessive by most standards.

It was almost immediately after we pulled up to the steps that led to the front door, that an older gentleman with clean-cut grey hair emerged. He held a briefcase in one hand and a stack of brochures in the other. It seemed clear that he was a realtor.

"Hello there," he said with a smile after approaching our vehicle, "was just about to close up shop. Are you here for the open house?"

"Yes, we are," Anthony said, returning the smile, "but we can come back another time if—"

"No, no, you wouldn't mind if we took a quick peek now, would you?" I interrupted my husband. Anthony gave me a look that implied my insistent attitude was a tad offputting.

"Not at all!" said the man, making it seem as though I wasn't infringing on his schedule. "I'm Quint," he said, "Quint Campbell. Allow me to get the door for you, miss."

"Thank you, Quint," I said, delighted that he didn't hesitate to accommodate.

"Appreciate that, Quint," my husband said, quickly turning off the engine and walking around the hood of the vehicle to shake the man's hand. "The name is Anthony. Anthony Young."

"Now that right there sounds like the name of a man who would be just the right fit for this home," Quint said with a smile. There was little question that he was a skilled salesman; still, he presented a sincerity that you just don't come across often. It was a sincerity that made it all the more puzzling why the gorgeous house hadn't yet sold.

"So, let me ask where the two of you are coming from?" Quint asked as he led us up the steps.

"Tennessee," Anthony said, "Nashville, to be exact."

"Ah, a fine city, Nashville is," Quint said, "I've never been, myself, but I hear it's an exquisite place for music fans."

"It sure is," I chimed in.

"Well, then I can see why you folks came this way; you're probably looking to get a little more peace and quiet."

Anthony and I glanced at one another. "Sure, yes, I suppose you could say so," I said, trailing off as I stepped into the foyer of the home. It was simply gorgeous. The floor was comprised of polished wood and topped with a large antique rug. The walls looked as though they had recently been painted white.

Aside from the rug, there was no décor of any kind. Usually, that sort of presentation wouldn't have helped with the selling of the house, but it made it easier for me to imagine our family photos displayed all over.

"What year was the place built?" Anthony asked, also marveling at the openness of the floorplan.

"Oh, it's relatively new," Quint said, "2001."

"Wow, only just over a decade, eh?" Anthony remarked. "That's good. Then it wouldn't need as much maintenance as so many of the others we saw."

"Ah, right you are," Quint agreed with yet another smile.

We were guided to the left, into a room that I imagined the previous owners would've used as a space to serve cocktails. I was delighted to see that there was another piece of antique décor left in the room—a grand piano that looked like it could've been at least a century old.

"Do you play, Mrs. Young?" Quint asked after noticing that I was eyeing the instrument.

"I wish," I said.

"Give yourself a bit more credit than that," my husband said before turning to the realtor. "She started taking lessons this past winter."

"Yes, well, I read that a great way to prevent aging is to learn an instrument," I said. "It was something I always wanted to do as a kid, but I just could never gather enough determination to see it through."

"I think most of us can relate to that, Mrs. Young," Quint said with a smile. "Please, don't be afraid to try it out."

By that point, I was only a few feet away from the instrument, so I figured I'd give it a whirl. I played an F chord. Truthfully, the only two chords I knew off the top of my head were an F chord and an A minor chord, so I took a few moments to alternate back and forth between the two.

"Beautiful," Quint said, "Just beautiful." He was right; however, the satisfying sounds were due to the quality of the instrument, rather than the skills of my fingers. It was while I sat on that piano bench that a variety of joyful visions flashed before me. There was one of Kellen laughing as he slid down the wooden railing while holding his father's hand. And there was another of Madeline and I admiring, through a magnificent window, the white caps atop ocean waves while we decorated Christmas cookies. It was as if my mind created a collage of our potential future. Right then and there, I knew we had to have that house; it was destiny.

"Honey? You alright?" Anthony asked, helping me out of my delightful trance.

"Huh? Yes, what is it?"

"Quint asked for us to follow him to the kitchen."

"Right, of course," I said, taking one more glance at the antique piano. The object had so much character; its rich history seemed to radiate from its very core.

With my arm wrapped around Anthony's, we followed Quint as he walked us through a high-ceilinged hallway that had three elegant, glass chandeliers hanging from it. We then emerged into the kitchen. I was so shocked, I completely froze.

Chapter 2

I couldn't make any sense of it; the kitchen was identical to the one that I had just imagined while I was sitting at the piano bench.

"What a view!" I heard Anthony remark, only it sounded like he was standing further away even though he was still right next to me. It wasn't just the kitchen, itself, that was the same as I had envisioned; it was also the way the yard and patio were situated overlooking the ocean. It was that moment that convinced me I had experienced a premonition. The windows were alarmingly beautiful, inviting in an enormous amount of natural light to expose the brilliant craftsmanship of the marble counter and spacious wooden floor.

"May we get a look at the yard?" I asked.

"Of course, of course!" Quint said, rushing over to the patio door, "wouldn't want you to miss one of the property's most attractive features."

As the door opened, I could immediately hear the poetic noise of the ocean. Although the view was stunning, it did worry me a bit how there was what had to be a thirty to forty-foot drop from the cliff onto a series jagged rocks.

"I know what you're thinking," Anthony said. "We'd just need to build a fence."

His words immediately dissolved my feelings of worry. Was he considering submitting an offer? My admiration for the property distracted me so much that I hadn't even heard if Quint and my husband discussed the listing price. Although I was curious about what that price was, I didn't want to risk anything that might rain on my parade, and I didn't want Anthony to make up his mind before we finished the tour.

It was as I strolled by myself closer to the cliff and picked a daisy from the lawn, that I heard a perplexing noise. It was very soft, but it sounded like several small seashells were continuously clacking against one another. It began to sound as if it was coming from somewhere beneath the cliff, but when I went to take a look, I saw nothing other than a steep stone staircase that led down to a small beach.

"I do need to warn you, Mrs. Young," Quint called out, "those stairs are old and have endured a bit of eroding here and there. Just be careful is all I'm saying."

"Right, thank you," I said, soon to recognize I could no longer hear any signs of the strange noise. I had no clue why, but there was something about that sound that captivated me.

The three of us held onto a somewhat shaky metal railing as we made our way down the steps. Quint was right to warn us of its deterioration; I could feel tiny fragments of it breaking off with nearly every step that we took. In all fairness, the abstract curvature of the slope looked like it would be incredibly challenging to build on, so I was willing to forgive that aspect.

"Allegedly, these steps were built long before any of the nearby residences," Quint said. "From what I understand, the beach down here was once used as a place for the community to gather."

"You don't say?" Anthony replied. "What would they do down there?"

"They'd probably sing songs and casually socialize," Quint said. "Honestly, your guess is as good as mine."

At last, after a very careful trek, we made it down to what I thought was a very cozy beach. There was something about the way a portion of the hill wrapped around it that made it feel like you were standing halfway inside a cavern. It was yet another aspect of the property that made it feel like it was straight out of a fairytale. It wasn't the sandiest of beaches, but the multi-colored, sea-soaked pebbles glistened from the sunlight. It looked like a motion painting. Something I found puzzling was the idea of an entire community congregating down there. It seemed much too small for more than ten people, fifteen at the most.

"Well, I think it's about time we begin our workout," Quint said.

"Workout?" Anthony replied, confused.

"The walk back up the steps," the realtor confirmed. "You're sure to feel it in your calves." He sure wasn't kidding. I got excited at the idea of finding out how my physique would improve if I climbed those stairs every day.

When we eventually made it to the top, we were taken to glimpse the remainder of the backyard. "Aside from the seaside view, the yard is my favorite feature. It extends for nearly six acres."

"It's extraordinary," I said, taking in as much I could from where we stood. There were so many trees and other kinds of vegetation that made it difficult to imagine what the yard looked like as a whole.

"We'd like to put in an offer," Anthony suddenly said, catching me completely by surprise. His words caused both my eyes and Quint's eyes to twinkle. "Do we even know what the listing price is?" I asked my husband, trying to make sure he wasn't getting ahead of himself.

Quint opened one of his brochures just to double-check the exact number.

When the realtor stated the price, I felt Anthony's optimism plummet. There was a moment of silence. "Well, I'm not sure why I hoped it would be closer to our budget," he muttered. "Still, it's a hell of a lot more bang for the buck than almost every other place we've seen. It goes to show that if you're willing to spend a bit more, you can sometimes get your hands on something extraordinary."

"That's exactly right," Quint replied, appreciating the positive tone.

"I don't know. What do you think, honey?" Anthony said to me. But I didn't respond; I was busy looking toward a section of the nearby woods where I could've sworn that I just saw movement out of my peripheral. It looked as though someone had stepped into the woods.

"Is someone else here with you?" I said to Quint. He looked confused. "There shouldn't be," he said. "The last couple left about thirty minutes before the two of you arrived."

I kept staring at the edge of the woods, but there was nothing there other than the gentle sway of tree branches.

"Ah, you probably saw a mother deer," Quint continued after noticing where my attention was. "I've been seeing a mother and her two fawns quite a bit ever since I started coming around here. I must admit they can be a nuisance, eating the flowers from time to time, but I do think they make up for it by adding some charm to the scenery." I thought it was likely that he was right, but it was hard to ignore how whatever I saw appeared to be walking on two legs.

"Yes, I'm sure it was just a deer," I said, trying to move on from the occurrence. The reality was that I was still preoccupied with the idea of that house becoming ours.

Chapter 3

It wasn't long after we had arrived back at the rental home that we received a call from Quint, informing us that someone had just submitted a strong offer on the seaside home.

"Okay, I appreciate you letting us know," Anthony replied into the phone. "Yes, I'll be sure to reach out if we decide to make a move." His spirits were noticeably low as he hung up.

"Surely, there must be a way," I said to him.

"Whoever put in the offer decided to exceed the listing price," he said with a tone of hopelessness.

Silence took over. It was as if the energy had been sapped out of life right before our very eyes.

"We'll submit a counteroffer," I said. "We can make it work if we truly want for it. I know we can."

"We'd need to sell all of our assets," he said. "And there's no question I'd need to rekindle my old hobby of day trading. Additionally, I would need to increase my client list, which would mean putting in even more hours every day."

"Yes, there you go," I said, "that's the spirit." Even though I did feel a bit bad about suggesting he works even harder than he already was, my excitement over the house continued to triumph. I watched as Anthony dialed Quint's number and informed him that we'd be submitting the paperwork for another offer in the morning. He was excited but visibly worried whether we were digging ourselves into a financial rut. But I knew exactly the thing to wipe away any nervousness, at least for the time being. I guided my husband toward the bedroom.

It was early the following day when we spoke to the kind old realtor and were once again bombarded with unfortunate news. He sounded sympathetic, but the other interested buyer made it clear that he was willing to offer as much as he needed to win him what I already perceived to be *our* home. Quint impressed that he no longer wanted to spoil our excitement, and that'd he'd be more than happy to assist us in finding something else.

The journey back to Tennessee was long and sad. But it was the strangest thing; even though I kept it to myself, I still had confidence that we would be moving into our seaside dream house. Although I failed to make any sense of it, the feeling was most certainly there. The more I acknowledged the strange feeling, the more the optimism returned.

When we went to pick up the children, Anthony's parents were quick to point out the contrast in our demeanors. They asked their son why he seemed so down in the dumps; meanwhile, I was acting bubbly as usual. After he explained the situation to them, I made a positive remark about how everything was going to work out just fine. I do think they were a bit pleasantly surprised to learn that we were having so much trouble finding a place out there; after all, it's understandable why they'd love for their grandkids to remain within driving distance. Both my husband and I tried to convince them to relocate to the east coast with us. They toyed with the idea but ultimately decided that the winters would be too severe.

It was the following evening that Anthony was out to dinner with a client, and I began plotting our next move.

"Hello Quint, it's Jessica Young."

"Ah, Mrs. Young, a pleasure to hear from you. I trust you made it back to Nashville safe and sound?"

"Yes, we did, thank you. I've decided I'm going to return to Cape Elizabeth tomorrow. I was hoping you'd be able to set aside some time later in the afternoon to show me what else you have in store?"

"I'd be delighted, Mrs. Young. Around what time were you thinking?"

"Well, let's see, my flight arrives at 2:14 PM. Would you be able to meet me at, say, 5:00? That would allow me enough time to get settled at the hotel."

"Perfect. Shall I text you the address of a listing? We can meet there if you like. I'm confident that you'll like it."

"Sounds lovely," I said. "Oh, and Quint, could I ask that you please direct all your communications toward me for now? My husband is rather busy for the next few days and won't be attending this outing."

Chapter 4

It was profusely raining when I landed in Maine. It was coming down so hard that I must've driven at about half the speed limit on account of how difficult it was to see the road in front of me. On the bright side, it allowed me even more time to strategize. It was after Anthony headed out for the day that I dropped the kids at a girlfriend's house. She had children of similar ages, and they always seemed to get along rather well. I sent Anthony a text once I got to Maine, explaining that I had a spontaneous craving to do a bit of house shopping by myself. I thought he'd understand because it wasn't all that unusual for us to take some time to ourselves. If anything, we both agreed it strengthened our marriage. The only reason I didn't tell him about it ahead of time was that I knew he'd try to persuade me to wait for the next weekend or he'd want to come with me right then and there. Unfortunately, I knew that neither of those options would help us to get what we wanted.

"So, what do you think of the view?" Quint asked soon after we stepped out onto the balcony. It was pleasant; it overlooked a meadow that was rich with flowers and surrounded by woodland, but it was no ocean view. As far as I could tell, you couldn't even hear the faintest sounds of the crashing waves.

"I should be honest with you," I said as the two of us leaned against the balcony railing, "we want that seaside home. That's why I came out here."

The look in his eyes implied that he wasn't overwhelmingly surprised. "Mrs. Young, I certainly understand your infatuation with that property, but I'm afraid there's just not much I can do."

"I'm just curious," I said. "Tell me more about the fellow who's so interested in the place. What does he do?"

"Um, well," Quint began, showing signs of feeling uncomfortable, "I don't believe I'm really at liberty to say, but I believe he's a hedge fund manager and owns an overseas company that must be quite successful."

"I see," I said, taking a moment of silence to look out toward the forest. "May I ask the man's name?"

"Mrs. Young, I truly can't say anymore. That would certainly be a violation on my part."

"Yes, I understand," I said, "not to worry. Do you mind if I run in and use the washroom? I'll be right back out to ask you a few things about this home."

"Of course," he said, "just head through the kitchen, you'll see it on your left."

After I made my way inside, I slid the door closed and began to walk toward the bathroom. When I got out of Quint's view, I stepped backward and peeked around the corner to see where he was looking. His back was turned, and he was leaning on the railing, admiring the yard. I knew I had to act fast if I was going to get what I came for. I glanced in every direction before moving into the hallway. There it was—the realtor's briefcase, resting against the bench's armrest. I didn't hesitate to dig in.

Suddenly, I heard the patio door slide open. Where was Quint headed? Was he coming to get something from his briefcase? I extracted a thin stack of papers and quickly folded them before sliding them into one of the back pockets of my pants. To avoid looking suspicious, I then snuck around the corner of the hallway and headed for the restroom. I breathed a sigh of relief after I made it inside and was able to close the door behind me quietly. I was too impatient to refrain from briefly checking the documents. After skimming through them, I was confident I had located the treasure; 'Marcus Davenport' happened to be just the name I was looking for.

It was right after I flushed the toilet and was about to turn on the faucet, that I heard what sounded like a large dog snooping and sniffing around the hallway area on the other side of the door. I just assumed the owner of the house had returned before the showing was over. When I opened the door, I fully expected to greet a friendly fur baby, but there was nothing there. I looked to my left, then to my right; there was nothing.

When I stepped back into the kitchen, again, there was nobody. I figured Quint must've returned to where I had left him on the balcony.

"Oh my gosh!" I yelped after feeling friction on my shoulder. I jumped and turned around to see Quint, appearing spooked by my reaction.

"So sorry!" he innocently pleaded, "This must've fallen from your pocket." He held up papers that I pulled from his briefcase. Luckily, they were still folded together, but there was still such an awkward feeling when he handed me the stolen documents.

"Yes, thank you," I said, trying to act casual. I put the papers back in my pocket. There was a moment of silence while I caught my breath. "So, what's the pup's name?" I asked with a smile.

"I beg your pardon?" Quint replied, speculating that he must've misunderstood.

"You know...the dog. Isn't there a dog here?"

"No," Quint said, "not to my knowledge. In fact, the current owner claims to be deathly allergic to animals."

"But...how could that—"

"Perhaps you heard someone walking with their pet along the sidewalk," Quint interjected. "Noise can sometimes travel in strange ways."

"Um, yes...sure," I said, still confused but forcing myself to move on since I had more work to get to.

Chapter 5

It was storming even harder by the time I made it back to the hotel. Quint had taken me through two new houses, and I acted like I was very interested in one of them just for the sake of wrapping things up. I told the friendly older man that I was eager to get on the phone so I could talk things over with my husband.

I typed 'Marcus Davenport' into the web browser and was somewhat startled by how easy it was to pull up information on the guy. It seemed that Quint's brief description of the fellow was on par. It wasn't long before I came across a photo of Marcus. Frankly, it caught me off guard. He was exceptionally handsome. Even though the photo was taken nearly fifteen years earlier, it was evident that he took care of himself.

I thoroughly searched the papers that I had taken from Quint's briefcase, looking for a phone number. After I dialed the digits, I nervously waited for someone to pick up. I badly hoped that I had just dialed a cellphone rather than a home phone. I was so relieved when a masculine voice picked up.

"Hello?"

"Hi, Mr. Davenport, I presume?"

"Speaking?"

"Hello, Mr. Davenport," my name is Holly Holmes. I'm an associate of Mr. Campbell's."

"Oh, hi," he said, "what can I do for you?"

"Well, you see, we found a few things wrong with the house over on Pinewood Lane."

"Oh, shoot," he said. "I suppose I should have my agent call you?"

"Actually, if you're still in the area by some chance, it might be easiest if you just come see for yourself," I said in a very flirtatious manner, hoping that his curiosity regarding who he was speaking to would take control.

"Um, well, I am a bit preoccupied at the moment, but—"

"It'll only take a few minutes, Mr. Davenport," I said, turning up my flirtatious tone even more.

"Yes, sure, if you think it's important," he replied. "Shall I head over now?"

"Perfect, I'll meet you out front near the fountain in twenty minutes?"

"See you soon," he said.

Are you enjoying the read?

I have decided to give back to the readers by making the following eBook **FREE**!

To claim your free eBook, head over to

www.LivingAmongBigfoot.com

and click the "FREE BOOK" tab!

Chapter 6

I stopped the car to check my hair and makeup one last time before I turned onto Pinewood Lane. I suppose it was the constant rain and humidity that created the fog, but it was so dense that I had to drive extra slow, which made me worried that Mr. Davenport was wondering if I had stood him up.

It wasn't long after I drove onto Pinewood that it seemed like the mist had intensified. Even though it was still daytime, I could barely see beyond the windshield. I was going at a speed of around five miles per hour when what I can only describe as a loud bark caused me to slam on the breaks. It was so loud that I knew whatever had caused it was extremely close. Suddenly, I saw the tips of what looked like antlers pierce the fog at maybe forty feet in front of the car. The antlers steadily passed by the hood of my rental vehicle. What had to be the strangest part about the whole situation was how the tips of the antlers appeared to be at least twenty feet above the ground.

Beep. The sound of someone's car horn went off right after a couple of high beam lights pierced my eyes.

Squinting, I looked into the rearview mirror and noticed there was another car right behind me. Surely, they were also having trouble seeing the road in front of them and almost ran into me. Though it was difficult to see any detail, it was apparent that a gentleman was behind the steering wheel. I wondered whether it could be Mr. Davenport. The commotion had caused me to briefly forget about the large moose or dear or whatever it was that had walked across the road in front of me. Regardless of the identity of the species, it was no longer in sight. I'll admit I wasn't the most educated when it came to wildlife, so, even though the thing was stunningly large, I assumed there had to be a rational explanation for it.

Both our cars slowly pulled into the driveway and parked alongside the fountain. The statue looked extra charming while smothered by the dense mist. When the man exited the vehicle, I was instantly stunned by his good looks. He was about 6'2" tall. His fitted khaki pants covered a pair of long and lean legs. He removed his aviators from his face, revealing his eyes matched his dark green collared shirt perfectly. Even though he had salt and pepper hair, it was easy to tell he had plenty of it, especially for someone of his age.

"Mr. Davenport?"

"Call me Marcus," he said as he embraced my hand. It felt so tiny and helpless within his strong grasp. Don't get me wrong; I suspected that he would be an impressive chap, but his presence made me feel bashful. To be frank, I'm not sure I had ever felt that shy when meeting someone for the first time.

"And you must be Holly?" he said with a smile.

"Huh? Oh...right, yes, of course!" I said, stuttering. I wanted to strangle myself for nearly forgetting the alias I had come up with back in the hotel room. If he hadn't mentioned the name first, I probably would've messed up and introduced myself as Jessica.

"Beautiful day we're having, isn't it?" the man remarked.

"Yes, I suppose it is...if you're into horror movies," I said, awkwardly.

Marcus chuckled. "So, shall we head inside so that I can take a look at these issues?"

"Sure thing," I said. "Right this way!"

Again, I wanted to slap myself across the face multiple times. I couldn't believe how what was probably the most critical aspect of my strategy had slipped my mind: the key to get inside the house. As if I wasn't already nervous enough.

I remember how I slowed my strut, pointing out various details of the property on the way up the steps. I needed to buy as much time as I possibly could to think of a proper excuse as to why I couldn't get inside. But my mind was blank. Suddenly, I had this very odd feeling that something wasn't right. I began to rethink my actions; for the first time, they were starting to feel utterly inappropriate. I figured my best bet was to come clean before this whole thing got out of control.

"Look, Marcus…I need to be honest with you—" I began to say as I placed my hand on the doorknob. To my surprise, the door was unlocked. My body language must've been so awkward-looking as I unexpectantly opened the door for the two of us.

"You were saying?" Marcus asked. "Honest with me about what?"

Suddenly, I gained a new sense of confidence. "I'd say the guesthouse needs a drastic makeover, wouldn't you agree?" I said, smoothly disregarding the truth that I was only moments away from revealing.

"I haven't yet given it much thought," he said as we walked inside the main house. "I just love the property so much that everything else is minor. It's this piece of oceanfront land that won me over as soon as I stepped foot onto it."

"I understand," I said, forcing myself to smile. I knew I had my work cut out for me. His words made it quite clear that he loved the place almost as much as I.

"So, tell me, Mr. Davenport, do you have children?" I asked as I guided him toward the kitchen.

"I do," he replied, "three of them."

"Surely, they must be excited about their future home," I suggested.

"Well, two of them are in college, and the other one is a freshman in high school. It would be a lie to say he's enthused by the idea of leaving his friends behind. Still, we have spent a lot of time in Cape Elizabeth throughout the years. They like it here."

"Ah, where is home?" I asked with a sympathetic tone.

"Jamestown, Rhode Island," he said. "It's a nice little community by the sea. Ever been?"

"I haven't," I said, "but I like the sound of it already. I'll have to add it to my endless list of places to see." I took a moment to glance at the fog-covered backyard through the kitchen's magnificent windows. I did this mainly because I wanted to use my peripheral vision to see where Marcus's eyes went when he thought I wouldn't notice. Yep, my prediction was correct; they veered directly toward my ass. I quickly turned to him so that I could catch him in the act.

"Lovely view, isn't it?" I asked, subliminally hinting at something other than the ocean. The man's cheeks turned a bit red.

"Yes, sure is something special," he said. It was at that moment that my primitive instincts took over. I walked over to Marcus and began kissing him. Even though I caught him by surprise, he didn't fight it one bit. It was no time at all before I felt his firm grip on both of my butt cheeks. The motion of his hands made it more than clear that he liked where things were headed. Soon, I found myself sitting on the edge of the kitchen counter. His shirt was unbuttoned, and both my red panties and bra were on the floor next to the rest of my clothing. It was as Marcus was kissing my neck that I began to hear it; that same noise that I listened to the other day while I was outside with Quint and Anthony. It sounded like seashells clacking against one another. It was such a strange noise, but what was even stranger was how, this time, it seemed like it was coming from somewhere inside the house.

"Do you hear that?" I said. But Marcus didn't answer; he was far too preoccupied pecking at the area around my belly button. "Wait," I said, placing my finger under his chiseled chin and gently guiding him up to face me.

"What's wrong?" he asked.

"Don't you hear that?" I repeated. It was when he looked at me all confused that I realized the strange noise had ceased.

"Hear what?" he muttered.

"There...there was this...odd sound," I said. "I heard it the last time I was—"

Marcus cut me off midsentence as he scooped me up and carried me up the nearest staircase.

Chapter 7

I was suddenly awoken by a familiar noise; it was the sound of my cellphone ringing. Still half asleep, I reached for the bedside table, hoping to grab the device. There was no bedside table. That was when I realized it was in the pocket of my pants, which were still downstairs on the kitchen floor. It hit me hard when I comprehended what had just happened. I couldn't believe I was lying naked next to a man I hardly knew. I managed to step out of bed without waking Marcus. The air now felt much colder than before, tempting me to wrap myself with the comforter before exiting the bedroom. The only reason I avoided it was because I thought it would likely wake my new friend and lead to a bit of awkward dialogue. As I tiptoed out of the room, I realized I hadn't even seen the second floor of the house that I was already so in love with. I supposed I was so immersed in the heat of the moment that I hadn't taken in my surroundings while getting carried up there. Though the bedroom had a lot of potential for charm, there was something undeniably eerie about it as I turned and looked at it from the doorway. It was weird how there was nothing in it aside from an old bed with white sheets, white pillows, and a chipped gold bed frame.

I tiptoed through the long hallway, marveling at how many rooms there were. I couldn't see inside any of them because their doors were shut and didn't bother to open them because all I could think to do was get to my cellphone. There were four missed calls, three of which were from my husband. I was discouraged when I realized it was dark outside and was even more discouraged when I looked at the time and saw it was 10:17 PM. That notion hinted that Marcus and I must've had way too good of a time. I intended to update my husband much earlier, but as I said, I had gotten carried away. I had to think of an excuse for having been away from my phone all that time. I wanted to wait until I was entirely by myself but decided I couldn't put it off any longer; Anthony was probably worried.

I was buttoning my pants when he picked up halfway through the first ring. "Honey, where have you been?" he said, sounding more concerned than angry. "I know…I'm sorry," I said as I quietly opened the door and stepped out onto the back patio. The mist had dissipated, revealing the reflection of the star-filled sky within the ocean below. Immediately, I was reminded of why I loved this place so much and why I had gotten myself into this whole situation in the first place. "Why do I hear waves?" he asked, still awaiting a response to his first question.

"I…I wanted to surprise you," I said, playfully. "I knew we both loved the Pinewood Lane house so much, so I flew back to see if there's still any way we could fight for it."

"But, honey, that's something we could've just done from home. I don't understand what good it would do going all the way back out there. I couldn't make any sense of it when I saw your text message. It was very vague, by the way."

It was then that I heard the sound of the patio door opening. I turned and saw Marcus stepping outside while he finished buttoning his shirt.

"I was wondering where you ran off to!" Marcus said in a playful tone. I immediately put my index finger to my lips, letting him know to shut up.

"Who was that?" Anthony asked.

"Oh, just someone in town. I'm at a local convenience store. I had the strangest late-night craving for ice cream."

"I see," he said. "I still don't know how you think we have a chance at getting that house. Our only shot would be if the buyer decided to back out of the offer."

I felt the muscles of Marcus's arms as he wrapped them around my shoulders. I was so worried that he was going to say something else that Anthony would overhear. I had to make up an excuse to get off the phone right away.

"Sweetie, Quint is calling me. Maybe he has some good news."

"Wait, you need to—"

CLICK. I hung up the phone before Anthony could finish his sentence.

"Why so secretive?" Marcus murmured as he leaned his chin on my shoulder. "Was that your husband or something?" He said it in a joking manner.

"It was," I said.

"What? Are you serious?" he asked. "You're married? Why aren't you wearing a ring?"

"Why aren't you?" I replied. He didn't respond. The expression on his face conveyed awareness that he was just as guilty.

"It's a long story," I said, breaking the silence. "We're going through a rough patch. Look, Marcus, I need to come clean. I don't work for Quint Campbell. I'm not even a realtor, and as far as I know, there's nothing wrong with this house."

The man looked so surprised, almost like he had just seen a ghost. There was a period of silence while I allowed my new acquaintance to take it all in.

"I...I'm not sure I understand," he said. "Surely, you didn't make those things up just to have sex with me."

"No, not entirely," I said. "I made those things up and prayed that I would get you alone. You see, this house is very important to my family. As I said, my husband and I have been having marital problems. One of the few things we've been able to agree on lately is our love for this house. I just know that if we were able to call this place our home, it'd renew a sense of hope for not only our marriage but for our family."

"So, you also have kids?" he asked, still trying to make sense of everything.

"I do," I said. "Two of them, a little girl and a little boy."

Marcus slowly shook his head. "You do know that you just seduced me and slept with me, right? Is that something you do regularly?"

"Of course not," I murmured, recognizing that it was showtime. I dropped to my knees upon the lush grass and activated the waterworks. With my face in my palms, it wasn't long before I felt a hand on my upper back. "My husband and I just haven't been on the same page at all lately. I caught him sleeping with one of his coworkers. But I can't blame him; we had been sleeping in separate rooms for a while now. The kids are so young, and they can keep asking if something's wrong. I just don't know what to tell them. But one thing I can't imagine telling them is that their parents are separating. It would devastate them." I took that opportunity to amplify the emotional breakdown. It was easy to tell that Marcus was thinking of a way to get me to calm down. Aside from feeling sympathy, I would imagine he also wanted to get off the property, given that he was technically trespassing."

"Look, I get it," he said. "Life is…well…it's difficult. But I'm sure you two will work everything out." Mr. Davenport was a skilled businessman, but he wasn't the most skilled at therapy. I stayed in place and continued to cry, staring at the ground.

"I wish I could be a better help," he said, acknowledging his inadequacy.

"There is a way," I gently replied. "You can retract your offer on the house."

"Look, I can't do that," he said, attempting to convey a façade of helplessness. "My wife loves the place too. She's very ready to begin life here."

There was another moment of awkward silence. I knew that it was now my chance to seize what seemed so rightfully mine. "Do you think she'd still be ready if she knew what just happened between us? Or what if the press were to find out?" I asked with an innocent voice as I looked up and locked eyes with him. I could feel his very soul tremble.

"You wouldn't," he said, clearly envisioning the chaos that would ensue if it turned out I wasn't bluffing. "I know you wouldn't dare. Then your husband would find out." His tone implied that he thought he had regained some leverage.

"I'm not too worried about that," I said. "As I mentioned before, we've had our differences and have both slept around. It wouldn't add anything new to the mix."

"You're lying," he said.

"Well, I suppose you can always try me," I said with an innocent smile.

"Look, how much money do you want?" he pleaded, "I can write you a check right now."

"I don't want your money," I said. "What I want is this house. Are you so sure you'd be around to enjoy it if your wife divorced you? Something tells me she'd probably kick you out." It was then that I knew I had won the battle.

I found myself sitting alone in the backyard, taking in the view and breathing in that remarkable ocean air. My dream had already begun to come true.

Chapter 8

I had only taken the first sip of my morning coffee when my phone began to ring. It was Quint.

"Good morning, Mrs. Young," he said.

"Good morning Quint, what do I owe this pleasure?" I asked, knowing quite well why he was calling.

"I have some rather fantastic news for you," he said. "The Pinewood Lane house has become available."

"You don't say," I replied, trying to sound pleasantly surprised.

It was just under a month later that the deal had been finalized, and we had initiated the move to Maine.

"Ice cream!" Kellen cheered as we pulled into the parking lot of a Cape Elizabeth creamery. Anthony and I agreed that it was important we get the kids off to a good start in their new hometown. Since they were both obsessed with ice cream, we knew this would be an excellent first step toward what was intended to be a positive change.

"Please be careful, sweetie," I pleaded with Kellen as I wiped his shirt while simultaneously paying the clerk. It was a Sunday afternoon, and the place was packed. It seemed that everyone in Cape Elizabeth had rushed into the shop to get a break from the summer sun.

All four of us were headed toward the exit when I thought I spotted a familiar face in the parking lot. No, it couldn't be. Why would Marcus Davenport be back in Cape Elizabeth? Could it be that his family had settled for a different property? I continued observing as a woman stepped out of the passenger side of the silver Mercedes sedan that he was standing near the trunk of.

"You know, I should probably run to the washroom," I said to my husband as I handed him my cup of ice cream. "I'll meet you and the kids back in the car."

"Honey, what do you mean? We're five minutes from the house," he replied, analyzing how it would likely take me longer to maneuver through the crowd than it would to get home. But I was already on my way. I'm not sure what I thought would come of it, but I most certainly didn't want to cross paths with Mr. Davenport, especially alongside my husband and children. Was it just because it would be excruciatingly awkward? Or was it because my gut told me that it would somehow erupt into some kind of nasty confrontation? The more I thought about it, the more I couldn't imagine the latter. Still, I wanted to avoid it.

It was as I reached the washroom door that I discovered it was occupied. Shit! I put my sunglasses on and discreetly stood on my tiptoes, trying to spot Mr. Davenport between the shoulders of the ice cream crazed mob. There he was; he and the woman who was with him were headed in my direction. I quickly turned around to hid my face.

"Been waiting long?" a female voice soon asked. I checked my peripheral and saw that only one person stood behind me. I turned and saw a woman around my age. She was stunning. Her mid-length blonde hair, sky blue eyes, and full lips were enough to draw the attention of any man. Who the hell does she think she is? It wasn't long before I noticed her wedding ring. There was something about her that got under my skin, but I was having trouble figuring out what that was. Surely, it couldn't just be the fact that she was married to Marcus. Why the hell should I care about that!? What happened the previous month was nothing more than a quick fling to get me what I wanted.

"I'm not sure what the devil is going on in there," I said before awkwardly knocking on the door. "Be right out," another feminine voice answered from the other side. She sounded stressed.

"My family just moved here," said the blonde woman. "We've spent a lot of time in Cape Elizabeth but only recently decided to make it our primary home. My name is Aubrey; Aubrey Davenport." She held out her hand for shaking. Now feeling a whole new level of awkwardness, I shook her hand. Her skin was so soft. Like her husband, it seemed clear she took great care of herself.

"Jessica," I replied, "Jessica Young."

"What a lovely name," Aubrey said. "Have you been in Cape Elizabeth for long?"

"No, not long now," I replied as I glanced at the crowd. That was when I noticed that Marcus's attention was now with the clerk. I realized it was now my best chance to get out of there undetected. "What a pleasure to meet you, Aubrey," I said, "I'm sure I'll be seeing you around!"

It was then that the washroom door opened and out stepped a young mother with her baby. "Wait, don't you want to use the—"

"Gotta run," I said as I began rushing toward the exit. "Just realized I'm awfully late for my yoga class!"

Chapter 9

I was overwhelmingly relieved when I made it to our car without running into Mr. Davenport.

"What's the matter with you, Mommy?" Madeline said. "Are you feeling okay?"

"Of course, my dear," I replied as I fiddled with my seatbelt.

"You sure?" Anthony asked, looking me directly in the eyes.

"Yes! I just had a little too much coffee this morning; nothing to worry about."

He then handed me my cup of ice cream, which by that point had turned into more of a smoothie.

The movers were dripping with sweat as they lugged one of our antique dressers up the front steps of our new home.

"Why don't the four us take a walk through the backyard?" said Anthony after made our way inside. "The weather is certainly too good to not take advantage of it. I say we try to locate a good spot for the bocce ball court."

"Bocce ball! Yeah!" Kellen cheered as his father raised him in the air and placed him on top of his shoulders. Our son had played the game at his friend's birthday party and couldn't stop talking about it ever since. Anthony promised him that we'd find a place for a court on our new property. It was adorable to see our boy get excited, especially given that he was usually so calm for someone his age.

"Let's go, let's go!" Kellen chanted from atop his father's shoulders. Anthony winced as his son tugged his ears in every direction.

As the four of us strolled by the guesthouse, I took a moment to appreciate our yard that ran alongside the ocean. It turned out that our new home came with a piece of land that extended just over seven acres. The house was beautiful, but it was the land that justified the cost of our purchase. As I watched my children frolic about soft green grass, I couldn't help but feel appreciation for my determination to ensure that the property would be ours.

It was quite a satisfying feeling to walk along your property, not knowing what you might come across. I was delighted when we came across an old, overgrown garden that was decorated with a collection of stone statues, similar to the fountain that was in our courtyard. The four of us walked along the unkempt path, laughing with each other while trying to name a few of the wide variety of flowers. I bent down to smell an oversized sunflower. Its scent was so potent that it nearly took my breath away. I kneeled before the colorful vegetation, almost in disbelief that this wonderland was ours to enjoy every day.

"C'mon kids, I think your mom's having a moment," Anthony said with a warm tone. "Let's leave her to it. The first one to find the perfect spot for a bocce ball court wins!"

I could hear the kids giggling as they ran back toward the entrance of the garden. I must've hung out in that area of the garden for around twenty minutes when I noticed the weather had drastically changed. Overall, it was still quite warm, but thick clouds now covered the sun and there was a cold mist in the air, not all that different from the way it was on the day that I won back the house. Suddenly, Anthony and my daughter returned right where they had left me.

"Kellen's not with you?" my husband asked, puzzled.

"What do you mean?" I said, just as confused. "I thought he went off with the two of you to find space for bocce ball."

"He did," Anthony said, "but then he was just...gone. Madeline didn't see where he went. We assumed he had run back over here."

A grim feeling washed over me. Though hard to describe, it was like everything had become overwhelming. I ran out of the garden, turned the corner, and nearly collided with my son.

"Kellen, honey...Daddy said that you wandered off. Please don't do that. None of us know our way around here yet."

"But Billy wanted to show me something," he said, calmly.

"Who the devil is *Billy*?" I asked. Anthony and Madeline arrived at my side.

"Don't run off like that!" Madeline scolded her little brother.

"Why would you do that?" my husband asked, concerned.

"Billy wanted to show me one of his favorite things! He said I could borrow it!" Kellen raised his voice. It was very unusual for him to protest.

"Sweetie…who's Billy?" I asked.

"My new friend. He was on the swing over by the woods," he said. At this point, I didn't even know we had a swing on the property.

"Um, okay. What does Billy look like?" Anthony asked.

"Kind of like me," Kellen said, pondering, "but kind of not. He has horns...kind of like Bambi."

"Horns? You mean antlers, dummy?" Madeline interjected.

"Madeline, stop it," I said, eyeing her. We all began to assume Billy was imaginary. But soon, all three of us spotted *it*.

"Kellen...what's that in your hand?" I asked, hesitant to give it a good look.

"Billy said I could borrow it," he said, innocently.

My jaw dropped as soon as I got a closer look.

"Kellen, put that down right now!"

To be continued...

WENDIGO WOODS: ANTLERS IN THE MIST

Conclusion

Thanks for reading the 1st installment in the series. Be sure to check out the sequel - *WENDIGO WOODS: A TOKEN FROM HELL* – now available on Amazon.

WENDIGO WOODS: ANTLERS IN THE MIST

Another Popular Series

If you're looking for something else to sink your teeth into, you'll love *SURVIVING SASQUATCH*. It's a thrilling true story. It is available on Amazon.

WENDIGO WOODS: ANTLERS IN THE MIST

Author's Note

Before you go, I'd very much like to say "thank you" for purchasing this book.

I'm aware you had an endless variety of cryptid books to choose from, but you took a chance on my content.
Therefore, thanks for reading this one and sticking with it to the last page.

At this point, I'd like to ask you for a *tiny* favor; it would mean the world to me if you could leave a review on this book's Amazon.com page.

Your feedback will aid me as I continue to produce products that you and many others can enjoy.

WENDIGO WOODS: ANTLERS IN THE MIST

Mailing List Sign Up Form

Don't forget to sign up for the *Living Among Bigfoot* newsletter list. I promise this will not be used to spam you, but to ensure that you will always receive the first word on any new releases, discounts, or giveaways! All you need to do is visit the official *Living Among Bigfoot* website and click on the "FREE BOOK" tab!

www.LivingAmongBigfoot.com

WENDIGO WOODS: ANTLERS IN THE MIST

Social Media

Feel free to follow/reach out to me with any questions or concerns on either Instagram or Twitter! I will do my best to follow back and respond to all comments.

Instagram:
@living_among_bigfoot

Twitter:
@AmongBigfoot

WENDIGO WOODS: ANTLERS IN THE MIST

About the Author

A simple man at heart, Tom Lyons lived an ordinary existence for his first 52 years. Native to the great state of Wisconsin, he went through the motions of everyday life, residing near his family and developing a successful online business. The world that he once knew would completely change shortly after moving out west, where he was confronted by the allegedly mythical species known as Bigfoot.

You can email him directly at:

Living.Among.Bigfoot@gmail.com

Printed in Great Britain
by Amazon